What do you think?

Poems to stimulate reflection and discussion in the classroom

Compiled and edited by
John Cox

Contributing Authors

Alison Carver   Paul Keeble
Ali Dee   Denis O'Gorman
Nick Fawcett   Susan Sayers
Michael Forster   Becky Silver
Barry Hart   W. L. Wallace
Val Hawthorne   Sarah Watts

kevin
mayhew

kevin
mayhew

First published in Great Britain in 2016 by Kevin Mayhew Ltd
Buxhall, Stowmarket, Suffolk IP14 3BW
Tel: +44 (0) 1449 737978 Fax: +44 (0) 1449 737834
E-mail: info@kevinmayhew.com

www.kevinmayhew.com

9 8 7 6 5 4 3 2 1 0

ISBN 978 1 84867 859 0
Catalogue No. 1501529

Cover design by Rob Mortonson
© Images used under licence from Shutterstock Inc.
Typeset by Angela Selfe

Printed and bound in Great Britain

CONTENTS

About the compiler/editor

Having spent rather a long time at various universities including Cambridge, Oxford and the University College of Rhodesia and Nyasaland, John was ordained to a curacy in the diocese of Liverpool in 1968. He spent a second curacy in an inner-city ex-slum parish in Birmingham and became rector in the same parish. After a five-year period at Church House, Westminster, where he was Senior Selection Secretary, helping to select ordinands, he was made Canon Treasurer at Southwark Cathedral and Diocesan Director of Ordinands and Postordination training.

Following four years as Vicar of Roehampton he moved to become Archdeacon of Sudbury in the Diocese of St Edmundsbury and Ipswich in 1995. When he retired in 2006 he was asked to be the part-time Diocesan Director of Education, a job he did for nearly four and a half years before retiring for a second time. It has been during these retirement years that John has been writing and editing for Kevin Mayhew, in between being chair of governors at a primary academy, playing golf and enjoying river cruises.

For details of all John Cox's books, please visit our website: www.kevinmayhew.com

Introduction

Teachers are increasingly being encouraged to help children to reflect. This is true for all schools but is especially true of church schools where the reflection can be given depth by putting it in a religious context.

The poems included in this book have been chosen because they are particularly suitable as texts that encourage children to reflect on who they are and their aspirations, on their relationships, the world about them, problems such as suffering, and the part they can play. In many of them the Christian content is implied rather than made explicit. Those in the sections on God and Prayer are more specifically religious but raise questions rather than seek to push a particular line. As the title of the book suggests, these texts are offered as a stimulus for children to explore what they think, how they feel about the points that are raised and it is suggested that they should be used in a very open way so that all children can enter fully into the discussion without necessarily agreeing with the assumptions behind the texts.

In primary schools, few of the teachers have specialised in RE but they are nevertheless expected to teach it. Some of them are very happy to do so and relish the opportunity. Many others feel less confident both in terms of the content and the way to go about it. It has been noted that this is particularly true when it comes to handling Christianity. Teachers may feel anxious not to indoctrinate children or some may feel uncomfortable to be teaching a religion they have consciously moved away from. In many ways it is felt to be easier to teach a religion other than one's own. This book offers a resource to assist teachers in opening up discussion of important issues in a way that neither ignores the religious aspects but does so in a refreshing and imaginative way.

Alongside the texts themselves, suggestions of questions and discussion points are also offered.

The poems included in this book have also appeared as songs suitable for children in various books published by Kevin Mayhew.

ONE

A group of thieves were waiting

A group of thieves were waiting
as a man came passing by.
They beat him up and robbed him,
then just left him there to die.

Someone help me! Someone help me!
Will you help in time of need?
Please, I beg you come and save me!
Won't you do this one good deed?

A priest came by and saw him;
thought 'My goodness, I must fly!
I'll be safe if I ignore him' –
so he left him there to die.

A Levite proved as heartless:
for he heard the poor man's cry,
but he hurried off regardless
and just left him there to die.

A third man heard him pleading,
so he stopped to find out why.
When he saw the man was bleeding,
he refused to let him die.

I will help you, gladly help you,
yes, I'll help you out, indeed.
Let me tend you, let me mend you,
I will be a friend in time of need.

Samaritan and stranger,
he could have just walked on by,
but he put himself in danger
so another didn't die.

Nick Fawcett

Jesus had been approached by a lawyer who asked him a tricky question about what he should do to gain eternal life. Jesus had turned the questioning back on the lawyer asking him what was written in the law (the law of Moses which was understood to be the laws given by God). The lawyer correctly said, 'Love God and love your neighbour'. But the lawyer persisted and asked Jesus 'Who is my neighbour?' Jesus then told the story of the Good Samaritan. A neighbour is obviously not just someone who lives next door. There is the neighbour in need and the neighbour who helped.

1. Look up the story in the Bible: Luke 10:25-37. What is Jesus saying about being a 'neighbour'?

2. What was so shocking about a Samaritan being the one to help the Jew? Can you think of an equivalent situation today?

3. Why do people ignore those who are in need?

TWO

A man he was praying

A man he was praying,
his eyes to the sky:
'Please hear me, I beg you;
reach down from on high!'
He called out for guidance,
for meaning, for love,
his thoughts turned beyond,
seeking help from above.

Truth's higher, it's greater,
it's stronger than you.
Respect it, explore it,
consider anew.
It's wider, it's deeper,
it's grander than me.
So pause then, and ponder,
just what it can be.

A boy he was gazing,
his eyes turned to space,
a look of amazement,
awe upon his face.
He gaped at the planets,
at Venus and Mars,
and gasped in delight
at the sweep of the stars.

A woman reflected
as life rushed on by,
and asked herself questions:
stopped to wonder 'Why?'
Asked, 'Why do we matter
and why are we here?
And why are the answers
we seek so unclear?'

A girl laughed for joy
at the world all around:
so brimming with beauty;
rich in sights and sounds.
She looked at the meadows,
the hills and the birds –
a life full of wonders
too special for words.

Nick Fawcett

Whether we are in need and seek help from God, or are amazed at the size and wonder of the universe; whether we stop to ask big questions about who we are or what life is all about, or we are just astonished at the beauty and intricacy of the natural world – it is important to think big, to ask big questions, to consider big possibilities. That's how we learn and grow and it is part of the wonder and mystery of God's universe.

1. Do you think it helps if you pray for help and guidance when things get difficult or confusing? Who would you be praying to?

2. What do you think the refrain (the part in italics) is suggesting?

3. The boy and the girl are amazed at what they see and it makes them wonder – about what?

4. The woman asks some very important questions. Do you ever ask such questions? Can you suggest any answers – even if they are not 'very clear'?

THREE

All of us are different

All of us are different, none are quite the same;
all have our ambitions, goals for which we aim;
different dispositions, different ways to be.
No one's just like you are; no one's just like me.

Some are good at English, some at doing sums;
some at playing football, some at playing drums;
some are great at dancing, some at history;
some find science easy, some a mystery.

Some delight in language, some at reading books;
some are would-be artists, some are budding cooks;
some are skilled at acting, some are born to sing;
some like certain subjects, some love everything.

Some find lessons easy, some find lessons tough;
some work every hour, some don't work enough;
some like chess or craftwork, some prefer to run;
some are rather quiet, some are full of fun.

Each of us is special, every one unique.
None should be an island, none accept a clique.
All have certain talents, each a certain flair.
Each a gift to offer, something we can share.

I will be myself then, look you in the eye,
treat you as an equal, hold my head up high.
We can teach each other, both have things to learn,
I need what you bring me; you need me in turn.

Nick Fawcett

When we come across someone who behaves very differently to us, who speaks a different language, who believes different things, it can sometimes make us feel we would like them to be more like us. And they are probably feeling the same way about us! But difference is a good thing. No two of us are exactly the same – not even identical twins. It is good to value ourselves – but equally important that we value other people who are different. Each one has a part to play, something good to offer.

1. Is it a good thing or a bad thing that we are all different? Why?

2. What particular gifts and abilities do you have? What gifts do you appreciate in others?

3. What does it mean to 'be an island'?

4. How special do you feel?

5. Why should we value other people?

All of us want to be winners

All of us want to be winners,
everyone likes to be first.
No one prefers being beaten.
No one is proud to be worst.

All want a moment of triumph.
Each of us hopes to be best.
No one would choose to be second,
conquered when put to the test.

All dream of being the victor.
All want to put on the crown.
All hope they'll end up promoted.
No one enjoys going down.

Only one person can win though.
Somebody always must lose.
Hard though it is to accept it,
sometimes we simply can't choose.

Whether you're top or you're bottom,
learn to greet both just the same:
not as a basis for boasting,
nor as a reason for shame.

It's easy to come across gracious,
when we're on top of the tree.
To smile, though, when we're defeated:
there lies the real victory.

Nick Fawcett

Some people are very competitive and try really hard to beat everyone else. To have the excitement of being a winner can feel really good. It can be anything – coming top in a maths test, getting a gold star for a piece of art work, winning a race or a football match, being the most helpful pupil of the week. Losing is not so much fun.

Some people behave really badly when they lose: they sulk or get angry. And none of us, even if we are not very competitive, wants to be a 'loser' – not all the time. But learning that we can't always win and being gracious when we lose is important.

1. How does it feel if you are never top at anything?

2. How do you think others feel if you are top at everything?

3. Think of one thing that you are really good at.

4. Which is more important: that you win, or that you did your best?

FIVE

Am I somebody's son or somebody's daughter? (Who am I?)

Am I somebody's son or somebody's daughter?
Somebody's nephew, somebody's niece?
Am I somebody's brother or somebody's sister?
Or am I just me?

Just me in this world would be lonely, I feel;
just me would have no one to talk to!
Just me in this world, I'd have no one to share with,
no one to whom I belonged.

Am I somebody's grandchild? Somebody's cousin?
Somebody's partner, somebody's friend?
Somebody's buddy or somebody's playmate?
Or am I just me?

Ali Dee

We all have a lot of different relations – even if we have never met all of them. Some of them may be very close to us – our mum and dad, our brothers and sisters. Cousins may be more distant and sadly some people have never known their grandparents. But we would not be the person we are without those relatives.

Just to be known as someone's son or daughter can be difficult. It could be like that if a parent is very famous – never to be known just as yourself but always as Madonna's daughter or David Beckham's son. Who you are is important.

1. List all the different relationships you have. What would it feel like without them?

2. Would you be the same person without all those relationships?

3. Which are the relationships you value most?

4. Is it possible to think of being just you without also thinking of whose son or daughter you are?

SIX

Are we all different or are we the same? (Are you like me?)

Are we all different or are we the same?
We all have two eyes, a nose and a brain.
But my eyes are brown and yours are green;
my nose is small and yours
is the longest I've ever seen!
Are we all different or are you like me?

Are we all different or do you agree
we all have elbows and shoulders and knees?
But mine are quite sharp and yours are round;
my knees are smooth and yours
are the knobbliest I've ever found!
Are we all different or are you like me?

Ali Dee

Every human being, every child, every adult is different. Each one of us is unique. Even when if we look very like someone else there will be differences. Identical twins can be difficult to tell apart but once we get to know them we can tell which one is which if not by their looks then by the way they behave.

But every human being is also very similar. We don't have any difficulty in knowing someone is a person and not a horse or a dog or a pig.

1. Does it matter that we are all different?

2. What would it be like if we were all the same?

3. Why do some differences seem to upset some people?

4. Identical twins look the same – what do you make of that? How can they be told apart?

SEVEN

Be patient

It's hard to be patient when you're in a queue,
with lots of people there in front of you.
Wait a minute, and then you'll learn,
it doesn't take long to get your turn.

> *Be patient, be strong.*
> *Be a little patient and it won't take long.*

It's hard to be patient when you've got the 'flu,
you've got a temperature of one-oh-two.
Take a tonic and try to smile,
it will only last a little while.

It's hard to be patient when you're feeling mad,
no one knows what a day you've had.
Don't be angry and shake your head,
it's better to try and laugh instead.

It's hard to be patient when things aren't fair,
and other people never seem to care.
Don't be moody and don't be sad,
and maybe your life's not quite so bad.

Sarah Watts

If you want something it's quite natural to feel you want it *now*. If you are hungry you want food *now*. If you are thirsty you want a drink *now*. Having to wait for essentials like food and drink can cause problems. But it isn't always essential to have what we want immediately. It doesn't actually hurt us to wait a bit. But it can feel frustrating. We can feel fed up, angry even. But that doesn't help.

Sometimes it just takes time to feel better and we have to be patient. Just being angry all the time will not make you feel better any quicker – probably make it take even longer. Learning to be patient – to wait graciously, is a hard but very important lesson to learn.

1. What things make you feel impatient? How do you deal with it?

2. Who makes you feel mad? What do you do about it?

3. What helps to stop you feeling moody or sad?

EIGHT

Believe in the future

Believe in the future of the world we all share,
where no one will be hungry and everything is fair.
A world of beauty, a world we must conserve.
Where all are treated fairly, and get what they deserve.

There's a bigger picture that we need to see,
this world wasn't just put there for you and me.
We should open up our eyes and try to find out how
we can make the future by doing something new.

Believe in the future, a future we can make,
where there are things that we can say and do for others' sake,
a world of justice, where all the human race
can work for wisdom, truth and love to make a better place.

Believe in the future of the home that we shall share.
The world belongs to everyone so greed should not be there.
A world of promise where all of us should aim
to know and love its family and treat each one the same.

Sarah Watts

We can sometimes take the world around us for granted. It's always been there, it's there now and always will be. And we can't do much about it. But that's not true. Although it is very old and very big our world needs looking after. Some of the things we do can damage it – beyond repair. We take minerals and oil out of the ground and they cannot be replaced. We cut down forests and burn fuels that damage the atmosphere. Many people believe that the weather is changing because of what we are doing. Some places are becoming deserts instead of being fertile land and others are being flooded so that no one can live there. The world has many riches to give us but some have a great deal and some have very little.

It is a beautiful world and we must treat it well so it has a future. We need to look after it, to share what it produces and not to be greedy, thinking only of ourselves. It is God's world but he has given it to us to look after and take care of.

1. What can you do to help ensure no one goes hungry?

2. What do you think is the 'bigger picture' that we need to see?

3. Would being loving and treating everyone the same make a good future?

4. What happens that shows the world is not a place of justice for everyone?

NINE

Can I give assistance?

Can I give assistance?
Help to get things done?
Let us work together:
two instead of one.

How can I help you?
What can I do?
Is there some way
I can bear your load too?

Can I share a problem?
Show I understand?
Can I ease your workload?
Let me lend a hand.

Can I make a difference?
If I can, just shout.
Say the word; I'm ready.
Let me help you out.

Nick Fawcett

There is an old saying that goes like this: 'A problem shared is a problem halved'. If someone is in difficulty it makes a big difference if there is someone there to give a hand, to share the problem. It doesn't feel quite so overwhelming if there are two of you to tackle it. Having to face a difficulty on your own can feel very daunting. We like to have help – and that means we should be willing to help others.

1. Is there anyone who needs your help today?

2. Was there anyone you noticed who needed your help yesterday?

3. What makes people hesitate to help others?

4. When did Jesus need the help of others?

TEN

Choices, choices

Choices, choices come along:
Is it right? Is it wrong?
Often things we choose to do
can affect others too.

Ask yourself, 'Will someone mind?
Is it hurtful, is it kind?'
Take a little time to say,
'Is this common sense and
will the consequences be OK?'
Choices, choices: when it's time
God of Love be my guide and in everything I do.
Help me to choose to be like you.
Help me to choose, help me to choose,
help me to choose to be like you.

Choices, choices there's no doubt,
shape the way things turn out.
So the best advice would be:
always choose carefully.

Barry Hart

When you have a choice to make you know that it will make a difference to you. So it's important to make the choice wisely. But your choices often make a difference to other people as well. Sometimes the choice you make feels fine to you but it hurts someone else. We can decide to grab the last biscuit on the plate when we have already had one and the person next to us hasn't had a biscuit at all. We made the choice to please ourselves without thinking how it would feel to someone else.

If we want to follow Jesus we need to make choices that are loving – not just for ourselves but for others.

1. Think about an important choice you have made recently. What were the consequences? Did it all turn out the way you had hoped?

2. What do you do when you have to make a choice?

3. What makes a choice a 'loving' choice?

4. In what ways does God show us how to make choices?

ELEVEN

Do you ever wish you could fly?

Do you ever wish you could fly like a bird,
or burrow like a worm? Well, how absurd!
Think of all the things you can do
and just be glad God made you 'you'.

Do you ever wish you could swim like a duck?
Unless your feet are webbed you're out of luck.
Think of all the things you can do
and just be glad God made you 'you'.

Do you ever wish you could run like a hare?
Well, wishing it, won't get you there.
Think of all the things you can do
and just be glad God made you 'you'.

Do you ever wish you could hang like a bat?
There's really not a lot of fun in that!
Think of all the things you can do
and just be glad God made you 'you'.

Do you ever wish – well, that's really enough!
To wish away your life is silly stuff.
Think of all the things you can do
and just be glad God made you 'you'.

Michael Forster

None of us can do everything. There's always someone or something that can do things you can't. You might long to be like them. You might try to do the things they can. But just think about all the things that you can do. There may well be someone who would love to be able to do what you do. It is always good to try to be better or to try new things but it's a waste of time just wishing your life away and never being glad about the things you can do.

1. Wishing is not always silly. Sometimes it can inspire you to do new or better things. Have you ever wished you could do something?

2. What are the things you are really glad you can do?

3. Do you like being you? Why?

4. Wishing can sometimes become jealousy. What do you feel about that?

TWELVE

Don't be scared of questions

Don't be scared of questions –
they're the way to learn.
Ask, and they will give you
answers in return.

Ask me why; ask me where;
ask me how, how, how;
ask me when; ask me what;
ask a question now.
Ask me this, ask me that;
ask me who, who, who;
ask me which; ask away;
ask a question do.

Don't fear seeming stupid.
Don't fear seeming slow.
Knowledge comes through searching.
Questions help us grow.

If you get an answer
but you're still not sure,
don't be shy to say so –
dare to ask some more.

Questions give us answers.
Questions stretch the mind.
Those prepared to ask them –
they're the ones who find.

Nick Fawcett

Have you ever been asked to do something and you've tried your best but you don't know how to do it? It can feel foolish having to ask when someone has trusted you with a job. But it's so much better to ask, learn what you didn't know and then get on with the job. Muddling through and making a mess of something just for the sake of asking is not worth it.

The great scientists are not satisfied with what they already know. They ask questions and keep on asking until they find the answers. That is how they discover new things. That's true for all of us.

1. Where do you go for answers to your questions?

2. What makes it difficult sometimes to ask questions?

3. How would you learn if you didn't ask questions?

4. Are there any questions no one knows the answers to?

THIRTEEN

Don't bear a load on your shoulders

Don't bear a load on your shoulders,
don't let mistakes fill your mind.
When you've done wrong, just admit it;
move on – the past left behind.
Don't let regrets come to haunt you,
don't wrestle daily with guilt.
Things you've done wrong can be mended,
trust and respect be rebuilt.

Don't think you can't be forgiven,
don't feel you'll always be blamed.
Own up and simply say sorry;
no need to still be ashamed.
All of us lose our way sometimes,
do things we later regret.
Learn to accept you are pardoned.
Trust that, and never forget.

Nick Fawcett

Have you ever missed a vital penalty in football or netball? You wouldn't be the only person who has. It can haunt you for the rest of the game and even the next game as well. You feel you have let people down. Missing key shots happens even to professional players. But they are good at putting it out of their mind – and just getting on with the game. They know it was a mistake but they accept that everyone makes mistakes and it doesn't help to keep dwelling on it. Team mates will forgive them and, hopefully so will the fans.

There are worse things than making a mistake in a game. Sometimes we do things that hurt others and we fear they will never be our friend again. But don't beat yourself up. Say sorry and move on. There is forgiveness. Accept it.

1. What do you do if you have made a mistake?

2. Does it make a difference what kind of mistake it was?

3. Do people always forgive you when you say you are sorry? How do you feel if they haven't?

4. Do you forgive yourself?

5. What difference does it make to know that God always forgives you when you are sorry?

FOURTEEN

Don't big yourself up

Don't big yourself up,
don't put yourself down.
Make known your achievements,
but don't go to town.
Don't trumpet your skills,
don't bluster and brag;
don't feel you're a failure,
don't wave the white flag.

Don't think you're the best,
don't think you're the worst.
Don't puff up your feathers
or else you may burst.
Don't talk up your gifts,
don't posture and boast;
don't think you have no skills,
or claim you've the most.

Don't claim you are right
and others are wrong.
Don't look down on people –
they also belong.
Don't think yourself great,
don't think yourself small.
Just open your eyes to
the value of all.

Nick Fawcett

People who are always bragging about what they have done, all the expensive things they have, the distance they went on holiday, aren't much fun to be around. It all gets very tiring. In the end you probably think less of them, not more. But the person who always says they are no good at anything, who are always undervaluing themselves, putting themselves down are not much fun either.

We might not do either of these things all the time but we probably do now and then – usually when we feel a bit unsure of ourselves. The bragging bolsters us up. We hope that by saying how useless we are, people won't expect too much of us and we won't let them down. It's not always easy but it's important to value yourself and value others.

1. How easy is it to be realistic about yourself?

2. Why would someone want to boast and 'big themselves up'?

3. What do you do if someone makes you feel that you are useless?

4. Are you always willing to appreciate the gifts others have?

5. How do you celebrate good things in others' lives?

FIFTEEN

Don't bottle things up

Don't bottle things up
if you're worried and feeling rough,
get things off your chest, talking's best
so, don't bottle things up.

Talk to a teacher, talk to a friend,
talk to Mum and Dad;
even if your problems still don't end,
you won't feel so bad.

Don't bottle things up,
there's no need to pretend you're tough,
people everywhere need to share:
so, don't bottle things up.

Don't bottle things up,
share your problems and sure enough
that is when you find peace of mind:
so, don't bottle things up.

No, no, no! Don't bottle things up!
No, no, no! Don't bottle things up!

Barry Hart

There are times when we can think that no one else will understand
how we feel. It may even be difficult to put it in to words for ourselves.
We can just feel down, fed up. Or sometimes the problems around us
seem just so big and the worries just churn around inside us. We feel we
ought to be able to deal with them but they just don't go away. We feel
worse and worse. It all gets bottled up inside.

It may not be easy but talking to someone can help. You may not tell them everything at first – you want to see how they react before you spill all the beans. You want to be sure they won't just blab it out to everyone else.

1. Why does it sometimes feel difficult to share things with other people?

2. Who do you share most things with, even secret things?

3. What happens if you do just bottle things up and keep everything to yourself?

4. How difficult is it to keep other people's secrets?

SIXTEEN

Everybody says, 'It's not my fault!' (Blame somebody else!)

Everybody says, 'It's not my fault!'
Everybody says, 'It's not my fault!'
Everybody says, 'It's not my fault;
blame somebody else.'

Adam said, 'I only do
what the woman tells me to.
She it was who tempted me
I'm quite innocent you see!'

'Not my fault at all,' said Eve,
'here's a tale you won't believe:
I was tempted just the same;
it's the snake you should blame!'

Poor old snake, he's out of luck;
nowhere else to pass the buck!
What a set up! What a shame!
Everyone should share the blame!

Michael Forster

This story can be found right at the beginning of the Bible in the book Genesis. God had told Adam and Eve that they could eat the fruit from all of the trees apart from one. But a wily snake had told Eve how lovely the fruit was, tasty to eat and in any case God didn't mean it. So Eve had taken the fruit from the forbidden tree and handed some to her husband Adam as well. They both ate the fruit. Perhaps they thought God wouldn't notice. But he did and he had it out with them. Adam felt guilty but he wanted to shift the blame on to Eve, it was her fault. But Eve didn't want to be blamed so she blamed the snake.

It didn't do them any good. God knew what each of them had done. Blaming others for the wrong things we do seems an easy way out. But it isn't. And it's not fair on the other person. Much better to come clean. Admit what we have done wrong.

1. Have a look at the story in the Bible: Genesis chapter 3.
2. What did God do about it?
3. What should we do instead of blaming others?
4. How does it feel if you are wrongly blamed?

SEVENTEEN

Flowers in the springtime

Flowers in the springtime
bursting from the ground;
calls from nesting birds
fill the air with sound.
Each a new beginning,
each a wake-up call –
promise for the future,
bringing hope to all.

Morning after night-time,
laughter after tears,
healing after sickness,
calmness after fears,
summer after winter,
sunshine after rain –
dare to trust the future,
dare to trust again.

Never stop believing,
never lose your dreams.
Never feel life's empty
though that's how it seems.
Though you're facing problems,
find it hard to cope,
life's still full of promise –
Never give up hope!

Nick Fawcett

When things are going wrong and we aren't feeling happy it can sometimes feel as though we will never be happy again. The future looks dark and bleak. But there can be new beginnings – think of spring after the cold of winter. The dark of night gives way to a new day. It is important to keep hoping that things will get better. Pains do get better, fears can be faced, sadness will give way to laughter again. It can feel as though it takes a long time but don't give up hope, don't stop dreaming of a better time in the future.

1. What dreams do you have? What helps keep your dreams alive?

2. What things that happen around you help you to dare to trust the future?

3. Why should we never give up hope?

EIGHTEEN

Forests are chopped down

Forests are chopped down for cattle grazing,
many creatures lose their place to live.
Animals are hunted to extinction,
we humans want to take and not to give.
Chemicals are poured into the rivers,
fish and plants, a thoughtless sacrifice,
people think of profit but they don't consider cost,
and the earth must pay the price.

We must care for the world,
we're here to protect it,
let all be aware that we should care
for this wonderful world
God has given for all to share.
We must share.

Roads and motorways are often gridlocked,
car emissions linger in the air.
Rubbish tips are full to overflowing,
can't human beings see this isn't fair?
Now's the time for us to take some action,
let's re-use, conserve and not deface.
So, for all the future generations yet to come,
this will be a fruitful place.

Alison Carver

Vast areas of the forest in South America have been chopped down so
that the land can be used for keeping cattle. It is of course important to
have plenty of cattle so that people can eat meat. But the big companies
that do this are not so interested in ensuring everyone has enough to eat
– they just want to make a profit. They are greedy. What is the damage
that is done by cutting down so many trees?

Human beings want so many things and everything takes resources. Some of these will never be replaced. Eventually they will run out. Farmers put a lot of chemicals on their fields to get bigger crops and more money but the chemicals can damage the rivers. Burning oil and coal lets off gases that many scientists believe is heating up the atmosphere and causing changes in the climate.

We may not suffer as a result of all this but future generations will.

1. Why is it selfish not to care about the environment?

2. What can you do to help conserve the planet?

3. What helps most to ensure there will be resources left for future generations?

NINETEEN

Give some thought to those you mix with

Give some thought to those you mix with,
those in whom you put your trust.
You may hate to be suspicious,
but at times you really must.

Facebook, Twitter, game site, chatroom:
is that the person who they say?
Though you're certain that you know them,
never give too much away.

Careful of that friendly stranger –
they may not be what they seem.
Danger sometimes lurks unnoticed.
If you need to, shout and scream.

Ask a parent, ask a teacher,
seek advice if you're in doubt.
Better cautious than mistaken.
Don't be rash and get caught out.

Nick Fawcett

It's fun getting in touch with friends on the phone or by the computer. There are so many different ways it can be done. And it can feel people are making a fuss when they warn you about the dangers. After all you are sensible. But there have been plenty of 'sensible' young people who have suffered because they trusted someone they met on Twitter or Facebook. The dangers are real and it is important to take precautions.

We are told to trust people – but we also have to be careful because some people abuse our trust. Discuss the signs that might make you suspicious.

1. How do you decide whom you can trust?

2. Who would you speak to if you were suspicious about how someone was behaving towards you?

3. What do you do to make sure you are being careful?

TWENTY

God gave me a body

God gave me a body;
not perfect I agree.
I wouldn't want another one,
it's good enough for me.
But now God says, 'You must take care,
take heed of what I say.
I gave you fruit and veg'tables,
so eat your five a day.'

Still, I eat beefburgers,
instead of fish and rice.
I can't resist those creamy cakes;
they're naughty but they're nice.
But still I think that God won't mind
if I have one today,
as long as I obey the rules
and eat my five a day.

Half the world is starving;
they don't have much to eat.
They can't grow apples, plums or pears,
they can't grow maize and wheat.
I wish that we could share the world
with children far away,
so they, like us, could eat as well
and get their five a day.

So, let's all be thankful
for what we have to share;
for all the fruit God gives us,
and say this little prayer:

'We know that you are watching us
and hear us as we pray.
So thank you, Lord, for fruit and veg;
we'll eat our five a day.'

Denis O'Gorman

St Paul talked about our bodies being like 'temples' – holy places where God is present (1 Corinthians 3:16). And he said it was therefore important to respect our bodies and look after them. Doctors also tell us to take care of ourselves – especially by eating the right things and taking exercise. Part of the trouble is that all the foods they say are not so good for us are among the ones that taste best. Some vegetables, like sprouts, can taste very peculiar.

There is also the question of over-eating and getting fat. Most of us have lots to eat – but what about the millions of children who don't have enough. We ought to be able to do something about that.

1. Why is it good to eat 'five a day'?

2. Which fruit and vegetables do you like and which ones don't you like?

3. How can we share with others?

TWENTY-ONE

God is good

God is good, he takes great care of us,
day by day surrounding us with love;
if we're happy or we're sad,
through the good times and the bad,
God is always there to lift us up.

Sometimes things don't go the way we planned,
all our dreams lie sinking the sand;
don't forget when you feel low,
God's a friend who won't let go
and he'll hold you safely in his hand.

Fill your heart with joy and laughter,
celebrate what God has done:
let's all praise our heav'nly father
that he gave us his Son,
and his love goes on and on.

Sometimes we do things that are wrong,
though we tried to be good all along;
when we're sorry then it's true,
God can make us good as new
for his love for us goes on and on.

And on and on and on,
on and on and on and on,
on and on and on and on and on.

Barry Hart

The Bible tells us that God is love (1 John 4:16). This could be the most important thing that can be said about God. It means that in all circumstances, at all times, wherever we are, whatever we do, however we feel God loves us. That is quite a claim. Does it mean we always get what we want? Would it be loving to always give us what we want?

1. Share with one another times when things have gone really well and you have felt very happy.

2. Share with one another times when things have not gone so well and you have felt sad, or disappointed, or sorry.

3. Has God felt close or distant? Does he feel like a friend who can help?

4. How does God show his love for us?

TWENTY-TWO

God is so much more

Charge up, plug in,
God is greater than everything.
Connect, restore,
God is so much more.

You don't need a mobile phone,
to talk to him at all.
He is listening all the time
and answers every call.

You don't need a satellite
to navigate the way.
God is always there to guide you
every single day.

You don't need an online friend
who's never there for you.
God is with you all your life
in everything you do.

You don't need the internet
or have to search online.
God knows all the answers
right up to the end of time.

God has power, greater, stronger;
no one understands.
He can hold the universe
and heavens in his hands.

Sarah Watts

We may not know exactly how smart phones or the internet work but millions of people use them. They just work (most of the time!). It is even more difficult to know exactly how God can be everywhere, know what everyone is doing, answer every prayer. But millions of people know it works (all the time!). We don't need clever gadgets. What do we need?

1. In what ways do you think God answers prayers?

2. Do you feel you can always talk to God and that he hears you?

3. Do you think there is anything God cannot do?

4. How does God show his power?

TWENTY-THREE

God sends a rainbow

God sends a rainbow after the rain,
colours of hope gleaming through pain;
bright arcs of red and indigo light,
making creation hopeful and bright.

Colours of hope dance in the sun,
while it yet rains the hope has begun;
colours of hope shine through the rain,
colours of love, nothing is vain.

When we are lonely, when we're afraid,
though it seems dark, rainbows are made;
even when life itself has to end,
God is our rainbow, God is our friend.

Where people suffer pain and despair,
God can be seen in those who care;
even where war and hatred abound,
rainbows of hope are still to be found.

People themselves like rainbows are made,
colours of hope in us displayed;
old ones and young ones, women and men,
all can be part of love's great 'Amen'.

Michael Forster

It must be terrible to have your home flooded. It doesn't just happen in other countries. At Christmas 2015, large areas of the north of England and Scotland were flooded. Discuss how it must feel to have your home, your street, your town flooded. What do you think helped the people who were flooded out of their homes? What gave them hope?

1. Look at the story of the rain and the rainbow in the Bible: Genesis chapters 6, 7 and 8.

2. Why is the sign of the rainbow hopeful?

3. How could you be a sign of hope to someone you know?

TWENTY-FOUR

Hand in hand
(We can change our world)

Hand in hand, we can do anything,
arm in arm, standing tall,
side by side, we can do anything,
we can change our world.

Using our voices, let us be heard,
calling for justice in our world.
Singing for freedom,
we can change our world.

Food and water, warmth and sleep,
every child deserves these.
Safety, shelter, health and peace;
we can change our world.

Ali Dee

There are lots of things that we can do on our own. Think of the things you most like doing by yourself. But there are many more things that we could never do without the help of others. List the first ten that come into your mind. 'There's strength in numbers' is an old saying. To try and change the world even in small ways requires the efforts of lots of people working together.

1. What are the things you would like to change about the world?

2. How could you help to change the world?

3. Who would you need to join with to start making a change?

4. Where are there children who do not have food or shelter or peace and who is trying to help them?

TWENTY-FIVE

How can I be a good friend today?

How can I be a good friend today?
How can I be a good friend today?
I'll be loyal, I'll be true,
I'll be kind and helpful too.
That's how I can be a good friend today.

How can I be a good friend to you?
How can I be a good friend to you?
I will listen, I will care,
and your problems I will share.
That's how I can be a good friend to you.

How can I be a good friend to all?
How can I be a good friend to all?
If there's someone on their own,
I can show they're not alone.
That's how I can be a good friend to all.

Alison Carver

Friends are very important. Think of all the things that you enjoy doing together with your friends. What would you miss most if they weren't there? How do you keep in touch with your friends? Is it realistic to try and be friends with everyone?

There are some people who seem to have no friends. What might be the reasons for that?

1. What makes a good friend?

2. How does it feel when you don't have a good friend?

3. Is it possible to be a friend to someone we don't like very much?

4. What about the person who no one likes?

TWENTY-SIX

How do you say, 'Thank you'? (Thank you)

How do you say, 'Thank you'
to a person that you love?
You sing a song, maybe just a tune
that you can hum along.
How do you say, 'Thank you'
to a person that you love?
You paint a picture, maybe just the colours
that you feel about them.

> *Say it in a whisper*
> *when no one else is listening.*
> *You can say it with a smile,*
> *in a twinkle of an eye.*
> *Don't say, 'Goodbye', 'Goodbye'.*

Tell them that they made a difference
to the things you did.
They made you smile,
they made you proud to be their friend.
Tell them that they changed the way
you feel about yourself;
they helped you win,
they helped you make it to the end.

Ali Dee

It can be very easy to take people for granted – especially those immediately around you – your families and friends. You can just assume that they are there and that they do things for you. Perhaps it is also true about your teachers. After all, isn't it their job to teach and help you? Does it make any difference when people get paid for helping you? Does that mean you don't have to say thank you?

There are so many different ways of saying 'thank you' – you don't just have to use words.

1.   What difference does it make if you say thank you?

2.   What difference does it make if you forget to say thank you?

3.   What is your special way of saying thank you?

4.   What do you say thank you to God for?

TWENTY-SEVEN

I can learn

I can learn about great artists' use of colour, shape and tone.
I can study famous sculptors, their creations set in stone.
I could learn of great composers whose music still lives on
and if I look in the Bible, I can learn about God's Son.

I can learn about the Romans, of their battles and success,
or about the ancient Aztec people's customs and their dress.
I can learn about the Tudors, King Henry and his wives,
but if I look in the Bible, I learn how God changes lives.

I could practise on the trumpet and learn to play a tune,
I could read about the earth in space, the planets, sun and moon.
I could study cloud formations seen in the sky above
and if I look in the Bible, I can read about God's love.

I can learn about inventors such as Edison and Bell,
I could read about explorers and their voyages as well.
There is so much we could study, on that we all agree,
but if I look in the Bible I can learn God loves me.

Alison Carver

What do you think you come to school for? Is it so that you can grow up and earn a lot of money? Is it so that you can do things that will make you famous? Is it so that you can learn? We look in science books or on science websites to learn about science. History teaches us things about the past. If you want to play an instrument you have to learn how to do it and learning how to read music usually helps. Do you think it matters if you learn about God or not? What sort of book is the Bible? Is it just one book? What do you know about the Bible?

1. What things do you most like to learn about?

2. Where would you look in the Bible to find out about God's Son?

3. How does God show he loves us?

TWENTY-EIGHT

I can play a part

I can play a part, and you can play a part,
let's start saving God's world.
Let's begin today, we'd better not delay,
let's start saving God's world.

*And if we all try together
then it's greater than the sum of its parts;
every man and woman, boy and girl,
let's start saving God's world.*

Walk instead of drive, it helps the world survive,
let's start saving God's world.
We all need to be conserving energy,
let's start saving God's world.

When we plant a tree it helps the planet breathe,
let's start saving God's world.
And it's good to care for wildlife everywhere,
let's start saving God's world.

If we bin our waste it tidies up the place,
let's start saving God's world.
Don't let out a scream, I think we're turning green!
Let's start saving God's world.

Barry Hart

Most people agree that the world is in danger for all kinds of reasons.
Resources like minerals and oil will not last for ever. We are polluting
the atmosphere and the climate is changing. If the temperature increases
by another 2 degrees, a lot of the world's ice will melt and huge areas
will be flooded. Many creatures and plants are in danger of dying out

because their environment is disappearing or has been polluted with chemicals. For every 4 tons of manufactured goods there is 80 tons of waste! Something needs to be done. It starts with us.

1. What could you do to save energy?

2. How could your school be 'greener'?

3. How much fuel would be saved if everyone walked to school once a week?

TWENTY-NINE

I could be a friend

If I felt sad or hurt my knee,
I'd want a friend to be kind to me.
It's not very much but means a lot
to know what a very good friend I've got.

I could be a friend if a friend needs me,
I'd be the best friend that I could be.
We could be friends to the end of time,
I'll be your friend and will you be mine?

I might not even know you yet,
you might be someone that I don't expect.
If I am inside or out to play,
I can make a new friend every day.

A friend is big, or can be small,
it doesn't matter where they're from at all.
I don't mind what friends I've got,
not very many or quite a lot.

Sarah Watts

Friends come in all shapes and sizes, all colours, all ages. Everyone needs a friend. Old people need friends, so do the young. It ought to be easy to make a friend but sometimes it can feel very difficult. Some people seem to be very popular and have lots of friends, others only have one or two. Which matters most: the number of friends someone has or how good a friend they have? Being let down by a friend can be very painful. Can you think of the ways in which some of Jesus' friends let him down?

1. What makes a friend special?

2. What does it feel like if you don't have a friend?

3. What do you do to show you are someone's friend?

4. Do friendships always last for ever? How do you feel if a friendship ends?

THIRTY

I could climb the Eiffel Tower

I could climb the Eiffel Tower until I reached the top.
I could cycle from Land's End to John O'Groats without a stop.
I could zoom off in a spaceship just to view the galaxy,
but wherever I travel God's love is still with me.

I might swim across the channel and land on Calais' shore,
I might go down in a submarine towards the ocean's floor.
I might rise up in an air balloon to view the distant land,
but wherever I travel, God's love is still at hand.

I could cross the dry Sahara and take a camel ride.
I could trek the Himalayas with a sherpa by my side.
I could take a trip around the world by land and sea and air,
but wherever I travel, God's love is always there.
But wherever I travel, God's love is always there.

Alison Carver

When we are feeling happy it can be quite easy to imagine that God is with us and loves us. When things are going wrong and we are feeling angry or anxious, lonely or useless, then it might feel God has gone away. That might be particularly true if we have done something wrong and are feeling guilty. Perhaps God is angry with us. Perhaps he has stopped loving us? Jesus tells us that God loves us not only wherever we go but also whatever we do. He just wants us to love him back.

1. Have a look at Psalm 139 verses 1-12. What are the differences from the text above? What are the similarities?

2. Can you imagine anywhere where God's love would not be with you?

3. How does it feel to know God loves you wherever you are?

THIRTY-ONE

I dream of a world full of peace, not despair (Dream)

I dream of a world full of peace, not despair,
a world full of laughter not pain.
I dream of a world full of kindness and care,
a world that is safe once again.

A world full of wonder, a world that is fair.
Here's my hope, here's my dream, here's my prayer.

A child understands how to give love away,
to feel for the heart of a friend.
A child knows a smile lifts the shadows away
and knows when to reach out a hand.

Ali Dee

Although the world is an amazing and beautiful place it can sometimes be a frightening place – just think of tornados and earthquakes. Although there are lots of wonderful and kind people about, that isn't always true – just think of bullies and cheats, of terrorists and criminals.

When things are going badly we long for the good things – for peace and laughter, for health and kindness. We can dream about a world where everything is wonderful but a dream will only come true if we all do something about it. Even such a small thing as a smile helps, it's a beginning.

1. What could make the dream come true?

2. Discuss what Jesus said about his followers becoming, as little children in the light of the second verse.

3. What was Martin Luther King's dream?

THIRTY-TWO

I may be small or big

I may be small or big or even in between,
I may have hair that's dark or gold as hay.
I may be very bold and brave or not so very strong.
I am who I am, is this OK?
I may be rich or poor, what will you say?
I may have friends and family in other different lands.
I am who I am, is this OK?

We're born the way we are,
a bright and shining star.
No one in the world is just like me.
I can make a difference
in the world this very day.
I am who I am, this is OK.

I may not be so good at playing basketball,
I may not have the skills to score a goal.
I may not be so good at playing any sort of games.
I am who I am, is this OK?
I may not be so good at adding numbers up,
I may not be so good at take away.
I may not have the skills to do what other people do.
I am who I am, is this OK?

Becky Silver

Some people don't like who they are. They are always wishing they were like someone else. Others think they are the best ever and no one could be as good as them. Most of us feel somewhere in between. We're sort of OK but would like to be a bit different.

Perhaps we should all be pleased we are the way we are but see if there is anything we could do better or any way that we could be better. It's not good to be always fed up with the way we are. But nor is it good to be self-satisfied and think we can never improve.

1. How does it feel being you? OK?

2. Would you wish to be more like other people? Who? Why?

3. How do you feel about others being the way they are? OK?

THIRTY-THREE

I may not be an Einstein or Isambard Brunel

I may not be an Einstein or Isambard Brunel.
I may not write like Shakespeare, nor even half so well.
I may not wow the pundits, they may be unimpressed.
But I'll be more than happy if I can give my best.

I may not hit the headlines, I may not be a star.
I may not be a whizz kid; perhaps I won't go far.
I may not like each subject, I might not pass each test.
But I'll be more than happy if I can give my best.

I may not be the top dog, the leader of the pack.
I may prefer the shadows, a seat that's near the back.
I may not be a student who stands out from the rest.
But I'll be more than happy if I can give my best.

I'll make my share of blunders, I won't get all things right.
I know not every project will turn out as it might.
I may not make my fortune, succeed in every quest.
But I'll be more than happy if I can give my best.

Nick Fawcett

Val Doonigan was a popular and very successful singer for over thirty years. He was a modest man and never said he wanted to be famous or very rich. He said he just wanted to be the best 'Val Doonigan' he could be.

Few people are going to be very rich or very famous or very clever or pop stars or brilliant footballers but everyone can try to be the best at being them and give of the very best.

1. Who were Einstein, Shakespeare and Isambard Brunel?

2. How important is it to you that you are successful?

3. What is the benefit of being ambitious? Who might suffer?

4. Is not succeeding at everything the same as being a failure?

THIRTY-FOUR

If a friend's in need and you just don't care

If a friend's in need and you just don't care,
if they're in a jam yet you still won't share,
if you only give what you've going spare,
then it's mean, mean – you know what I mean.

If you ditch a friend when they're feeling low,
if you're asked to help and you just say no,
if you turn your back when they need you so,
then it's mean, mean – you know what I mean.

If a friend is stuck and they can't get through,
if you walk away when they're in a stew,
if they need a hand and you just say 'Shoo!'
Then it's mean, mean – you know what I mean.

Give that extra bit, go that extra mile,
offer what you can with a cheerful smile,
show a loving heart, make it all worthwhile –
don't be mean, mean – you know what I mean.

Nick Fawcett

Jimmy had twenty sweets but when his friend Tom asked him for one, Jimmy refused. 'You're mean,' said Tom. Jane was really upset when she lost her ipod but Michelle just laughed at her for crying. She was being mean. Discuss what you would consider as being 'mean'.

1. Why might you not care if a friend was in need?

2. Why is it mean only to give what you've got spare?

3. What did Jesus mean when he told his followers to 'go the extra mile'?

4. Are your friends the only ones you should help? In what way is helping only your friends not good enough?

THIRTY-FIVE

If I can be strong

If I can be strong, admit when I'm wrong,
if I'm not too proud to say I'm sorry.
If it matters to me too, it's not fair for you;
we can learn to stand up for each other.

We will have peace, we will have harmony.
We can build our lives together.
We will have peace, we will have harmony.
We will learn to live as one.

If we can make up our minds, it's OK to be kind;
we've been told that we should love each other.
If I do love someone else the way I love myself,
if I treat you like I would be treated.

Peace is so much more than the absence of war,
it's a flower growing on the tree of justice.

Paul Keeble

How other people feel is important. It matters if we hurt them or annoy them – even when that is unintentional. All the more reason then to say sorry. It matters if we understand that a person is not being treated fairly and we try to do something about it. It isn't being soft or a cissy to be kind – kind is cool.

Jesus said we should love one another but he knew it isn't always easy. Some people think that they can only love the people they like. Do you agree? Is treating someone in a loving way necessarily the same as liking them?

1. Why does it feel difficult to admit we are wrong or to say sorry?

2. What prevents us from having peace?

3. What does it mean to love others as we love ourselves?

THIRTY-SIX

If I make things up,
if I tell you lies

If I make things up, if I tell you lies,
then a shaking head should be no surprise.
If I don't come clean; hide the facts from sight;
then you won't believe what I say is right.

> *Trust what I say, trust what I do –*
> *you only will if you know it's true.*

If I lead you on, and my words deceive,
then I can't complain when you won't believe.
If I spin a yarn, if I twist the truth,
then it's down to me if you hit the roof.

Why not spell it out? Why not tell it straight?
Get it off your chest? Clear it off the plate?
Always tell the truth – never mind the rest.
Yes, it may be hard, but you know it's best.

Nick Fawcett

There's a story about a boy who used to frighten all the people in the village where he lived by running down the street shouting, 'Wolf! Wolf!' People would run into their houses to escape the wolf. But there was no wolf. The boy was lying. He kept doing it but no wolf appeared. Eventually the people realised he was just lying. They could not trust him. One day the boy really did see a wolf and shouted to all the villagers. They took no notice. And they were very upset when the wolf killed their sheep and chased the children.

1. When does a lie feel easier than the truth?

2. Why is telling the truth so important?

3. How much would you trust others if you know they tell lies?

4. Is there ever a good reason for not telling the truth?

THIRTY-SEVEN

If only we'd stop,
and look, and see

If only we'd stop, and look, and see,
we would be rejoicing constantly,
celebrating all the world can give,
all that makes each day a joy to live.

Let's learn to celebrate, to laugh and sing,
give thanks with grateful hearts for everything.
Let's learn to recognise how blessed we are.
Let's dance a joyful jig, let's shout, 'hurrah!'

If we'd count our blessing as we should,
we would see how rich life is, and good.
Far from ever moaning at our lot,
we would leap for joy at all we've got.

If we look about us for a while,
we will find so much to make us smile:
gifts to brighten up the darkest day,
special more than words can ever say.

Nick Fawcett

The world is never exactly the way we would like it. Things don't work out every time the way we want. We don't always get what we ask for. But there are still so many things to be grateful for. There is so much to be glad about. Just think of all the things you do have. You have enough to eat. You don't sleep in the street, you don't have to go begging to have a pair of shoes. You don't have to work from dawn till dusk making bricks or scavenging on the refuse tips. Think of the good things you have and imagine what it would be like to live with no home, no one who loved you, no school, no possessions, no spare clothes, no parties or treats.

1. Make a list of all the things you are grateful for. Discuss them with others.

2. What would you like to celebrate today? Something you have done? Something someone else has done?

3. Think of all the things you have that a refugee child does not have.

THIRTY-EIGHT

If you were stripy or dotty (Stripy dotty friends)

If you were stripy or dotty, I wouldn't mind at all
just so long as you'd play and be my friend.
If you were lumpy or bumpy, or teeny tiny small,
I still think we'd be friends after all.

If you were kind, I wouldn't mind
if you spoke 'Hinky ponky doo'.
If you shared and showed you cared;
it wouldn't matter if your hands and feet were blue!

If you were fun to be around
it wouldn't matter if you grew
fifty ears upon your head;
it wouldn't matter if your hands and feet were blue!

Yes, we'd be friends, best of friends,
doesn't matter if we're different.
Stripy, dotty, lumpy, bumpy, blue friends are best!

Ali Dee

Some people seem to get quite anxious about mixing with other people who are different to them – people from other countries, people who speak a different language, people who have a different colour, people who follow a different religion. How much do these things matter to you? Do you think they should matter? If someone is a really good friend, differences don't matter. But what if someone is different and you don't like them?

1. Would anything matter about someone so long as they were your friend?

2. Some people are different and have no friends. What should you do?

3. What is there about you that feels different?

THIRTY-NINE

If you're feeling kind of lonely

If you're feeling kind of lonely,
if you're left out in the cold;
if you long to join the party
but you're kept outside the fold;
think instead of those you're close to,
friends with whom you get along;
think of all you share together
and remember you belong.

If you feel yourself unwelcome,
like a stranger in the crowd;
if you yearn to be accepted
but it feels you're not allowed;
think of parents, brothers, sisters,
uncles, aunties – love so strong –
think of all who count you special
and remember you belong.

If you're not quite sure you matter,
and yet no one seems to care;
if the universe feels empty
and you wonder why you're there;
think again, and know you're precious –
should you question that, you're wrong.
Take your place within creation
and remember you belong.

Nick Fawcett

Thousands of children were asked what matters most to them when they are at school. How would you have answered that question?

The answer that came up most often was, 'I want to belong.' Discuss what that might mean for you and for each other.

1. How does it feel when you are left out of things?

2. What could you do to make sure no one in your class is left out in the cold?

3. What do you belong to?

4. How has God shown that you are precious to him?

FORTY

If you're feeling worried, troubled

If you're feeling worried, troubled,
not sure where to turn,
here's a lesson we've been given:
one we need to learn.

Life is more than food and clothing,
what we eat and wear.
Think about what really matters;
for the rest, don't care.

Think of flowers in the meadow,
think of birds upon the nest;
these don't brood on their appearance
yet we can't but be impressed.

Hours of fretting will not help us;
end our doubts, allay our fears.
Worry only saps the spirit.
Self-assurance disappears.

Take each moment as you find it.
Face your problems one by one.
Trust your God to see you through them.
Life has only just begun!

Nick Fawcett

Often our worries are about basic things like what we are going to wear, what we will eat, how we look. They feel quite important at the time and worrying can get us down. The problems just seem to mount up. In countries where food is short and people are poor these things matter even more. Jesus knew this and told his friends that it would be good if they stopped getting so anxious about these things. They should trust God. But we have to ask: does God always supply everybody's needs? People do starve. People can be so poor they have no money for clothes. Doesn't he care about them?

God does provide enough for everybody if only we would share them out. God wants those who have a lot to be willing to share with those who have little. We have to take responsibility. That's how we all learn to be more like the kind of people God would want us to be.

1. Look at what Jesus said about this. (Matthew 6:25-33)

2. What do you think 'really matters'?

3. Not worrying and not planning are different. In what ways?

4. How do you think God helps you to face your problems?

FORTY-ONE

In this world it's not hard to spot

In this world it's not hard to spot,
some have little but some have lots,
some are 'haves' and some have-nots':
it's a world of difference.
Look around and you will see
some folk living in luxury,
some exist in poverty:
it's a world of difference.

It isn't wrong to have good things,
enjoy the blessings that God brings
but only stop a while to think
he gave us lots so we can share.
Help us to give as well as take,
help us love for pity's sake,
so that together we can make:
a world of difference.

Crops are failing for lack of rain,
children crying with hunger pains
while we're throwing food away:
it's a world of difference.
Shopping centres which rarely close,
price reductions and bargain clothes:
but the child who made them knows:
it's a world of difference.

In the cities hotels rise
ever higher into the skies,
people will sleep rough tonight:
it's a world of difference.

So the needy are everywhere,
near and far there are not fair shares;
give us hearts and hands to care:
it's a world of difference.

Barry Hart

Try to imagine a world where everything was the same – the countryside all looked the same, the weather everywhere was always the same, the people were all the same, they dressed the same, they spoke the same, they all did the same job. What would you make of a world like that? Difference can be good.

But some differences are unfair and that's not good. What can be done about it?

1. Why is there poverty when so many are rich?

2. What do you think about the use of child labour?

3. How can the world's hungry be fed? What difference could you make?

FORTY-TWO

Is there a reason behind why we're here?

Is there a reason behind why we're here?
Did we just happen? Just somehow appear?
Does life have meaning, some purpose, some goal?
Are we just bodies, or have we a soul?

Look at the world
and what do you see?
Is there more to it –
a great mystery?

Are we just bundles of atoms and cells –
what chemistry, physics, biology tells?
Are we mere signals that buzz in the brain?
Is truth so simple, so stark and so plain?

Can we make sense of the things that take place –
the evil and sorrow that so many face?
Faced by injustice, disaster and grief,
can we keep hold of some faith, some belief?

Some say God loves us, that each day he acts,
others claim faith doesn't fit with the facts.
Weigh up the questions and see what you find.
You must decide – need to make up your mind.

Nick Fawcett

Discuss how you think the world came into being. What started it all? Science has answers. But so do all the religions of the world – often in the form of stories. They may not give us the facts about 'how' but they try to answer even more difficult questions: 'Why did it all start? What does it all mean? What's the purpose?' The stories religions tell, like the story of Adam and Eve in the Bible (see the book of Genesis chapters 1-3) give us clues into what in the end is a mystery – meaning we don't know all the answers, no one does.

1. What purpose or meaning do you think the world has?

2. How do you understand what is meant by 'soul'?

3. Do you think it is possible to believe in a God who loves us when there is so much suffering in the world?

FORTY-THREE

It's good to pray

It's good to pray a little every day,
because we know that God is very near.
And if we pray
then in a special way,
He hears and answers our prayer.

We'll tell God all about our families and friends,
ask him to keep them in his care.
We'll tell him all about those funny little things
that might worry or frighten us today.

We'll close our eyes and picture all who are in need,
those who are hungry or alone.
We'll pray for all who are unhappy or unwell
and that those who work among them will be strong.

Val Hawthorne

We can pray when we are all together – for example, in Collective Worship. Or we can pray when we are on our own. Sometimes a prayer has words that we learn off by heart and use often – prayers like the Lord's Prayer, or a prayer before we have a meal. But we can make our own prayers up – just saying what we feel to God.

There are different kinds of prayer, e.g.

Adoration – when we worship and praise God.

Confession – when we say we are sorry.

Thanksgiving – when we are grateful for all God gives us.

Supplication – when we pray for others as well as for ourselves.

1. What do you think is the special way that God hears and answers prayer?

2. Can we say prayers at any time?

3. Who do you think are in particular need of our prayers today?

4. Is prayer enough?

FORTY-FOUR

Let's be green

Let's be green in our school today,
let's think about the world of tomorrow.
What can we do to be green today
that will help the world tomorrow?
We'll keep our eyes open all day long,
as we go around school we'll see what's wrong.
Computers on standby – that's not right;
and we mustn't forget to turn off the light.

Let's care for God's creation,
and try to keep tomorrow bright,
we'll think of all the ways we can help the world,
and start by turning off the light.

Let's be green in our school today,
let's think about the world of tomorrow.
How many ways are we green today
that will help the world of tomorrow?
We'll try to keep thinking all day long,
and we'll notice the things we know are wrong.
Recycle our paper – that's quite right,
and we mustn't forget to turn off the light.

Let's be green in our school today,
let's think about the world of tomorrow.
How can we work to be green today
that will help the world of tomorrow?
We'll try to keep looking all day long,
and we'll soon find some ways to change what's wrong.
Save energy now – we know that's right,
so we mustn't forget to turn off the light!

Val Hawthorne

A lot of people talk about being 'green' these days. At one time if it was said that someone was being 'green' it meant that they were being a bit stupid. But not now. Discuss why the colour green is chosen to describe people and organisations who are trying to protect our world. What would happen if all the green things disappeared?

1. What does your school do to be green?

2. Is there more that could be done?

3. Why is it important that we think about tomorrow today?

FORTY-FIVE

Let's have a minute's silence

Let's have a minute's silence
for all who died in war.
For they were all God's children
and hated what they saw;
the planes and ships on which men died,
the tanks and rifles too.
But they were all God's people,
just like me and you.

So each and every nation
remembers them with pride.
For they believed when fighting
that God was on their side.
But God looks down when people fight,
from heaven, high above
and says, 'You are my people,
all you need is love.'

It's true we must remember
the sacrifice they made,
to rid the world from evil
and what a price they paid.
May angels take them all to God;
now free from death and pain.
As now they are together,
peace may come again.

Denis O'Gorman

It is traditional in Britain to keep silence for a couple of minutes each
year at 11 am on 11 November. Do you know why this time and day was
chosen? It was to do with the end of the first World War in 1918. Stopping

doing what we are doing and keeping quiet gives us the opportunity to remember those who have died because of war – soldiers and sailors and airmen, but also all the civilians. Wars are still happening. People are still dying – people who are enemies, people who never wanted there to be a war. It is sad for all of them. They all need to be thought about. If we all thought a bit more about the sadness war brings we would work harder to make sure there was peace.

1. What are the reasons for nations to go to war?
2. Jesus told his followers to love their enemies. How do you feel about that?
3. What reasons are there for being a pacifist?
4. Does God take sides in a war?

FORTY-SIX

Let's take care of our body

Let's take care of our body
and look after our health;
praising God for the way we're made,
let's take care of ourself.

We've got legs to jump and run,
we've got hands to catch and throw.
Hey! This exercising's fun.
On your marks! Now get set! GO.

Food is fuel for our body,
keeps us moving along;
'five-a-day' is a real good way,
keeps us healthy and strong.

Thank you God for our bodies,
help us keep in good shape;
then we'll know as our bodies grow
everything will feel great!
Yeah! everything will feel great!
Yeah! everything will feel great!

Barry Hart

- Every day someone dies as a result of being overweight. 1 in 11 deaths in Britain is caused by obesity.

- Every year nearly half a million men and women die as a result of smoking.

- Every day more than 25 people die as a result of drinking too much alcohol.

- Every day 10 people die as a result of taking drugs.

Nearly all of these deaths could have been avoided. It makes you think. Taking care of what you do with your body matters – not because that's what someone has told you but because it makes a difference to how you feel, how well you are.

1. Why is it important to look after your body?

2. What do you need as well as the right food?

3. What different ways might you get the exercise you need?

FORTY-SEVEN

Life is for living now

Life is for living now;
not moaning or groaning,
avoiding, disowning:
life is for living now!

Life is for living now;
not killing or caging,
destroying or grasping:
life is for living now!

Life is for living now;
for feeling and thinking,
for growing and finding:
life is for living now!

Life is for living now;
for praying and serving,
for living and loving:
life is for living now!

Life is for living now;
for healing and freeing,
rejoicing and dancing:
life is for living now!

W.L Wallace

It's good if we can all say: 'It's great to be alive.'

It's good to make the most of what we have. Some people don't have it easy: they are anxious or ill, they live in fear or in prison, they just don't know how to enjoy life.

Some people think that the only way to make life good is to have everything they want and to keep everything to themselves. Others suggest that to make life good you need to think of others, to share what you have. What do you think?

1. What things make living now good? What makes it bad?

2. Who shows us what living life well is like?

3. What piece of 'good living' will you try to do today?

FORTY-EIGHT

Many people worship

Many people worship; many people pray,
many seek God's presence, each in their own way.
Some through church or temple, some through mosque instead –
seeking deeper meaning, asking to be led.

Who do you worship?
Who do you adore?
Can we look beyond us?
Is there nothing more?

Some say God is distant, others that he's near;
some claim we can find him by our sides, right here.
Some seek him around us; some in things above;
some in creeds and doctrine; some in deeds of love.

Some seek God through silence; some through many words;
some commune with nature; mountains, forests, birds.
Some use meditation; others songs of praise;
some say words of Scripture best reveal his ways.

Some deny God's presence; some sit on the fence.
Some say faith is foolish, claim it makes no sense.
Have you made your mind up? Have you made your choice?
Will you keep on seeking, open to God's voice?

Nick Fawcett

Some people suggest that we should never talk about religion. Religion is just a matter of what you believe and you should keep that to yourself. Discussing religion, they say, always ends up in an argument because no one can prove if there is a God or not and no one knows for certain exactly what God is like (if there is one). Do you think it matters if we talk about religion or not? In what ways might it be a good thing to find out what others believe?

1. Is there a 'right' way to seek God?

2. What do you find is the best way for you?

3. If you have not yet made up your mind, what would help you to do so?

4. Do you think it matters whether people believe in God or not?

FORTY-NINE

My Granny and Granddad

My Granny and Granddad are good fun,
I love to hear all their stories.
Since Granny and Granddad both were young
the world is different, it sure is.

This old world goes spinning round:
always been a place of ups and downs;
gonna build my life on solid ground,
my God never changes.
This old world clearly shows:
always been a place of high and lows;
gonna put my trust in him I know
my God never changes.

Nobody had mobiles or CDs
or games to play on computers.
They didn't watch films on DVDs,
these things were all in the future.

When Granny and Granddad both grew up
their meals weren't kept in a freezer.
You didn't mix soups up in a cup
or order take-away pizza.

The clothes they wore were not the same;
the style, the colour, the pattern.
But Granny says they'll be back again
and called the trendiest fashion.

Barry Hart

'There is one thing that is always the same and that is change' – so the saying goes. Whatever else happens we can be sure that things will change. We grow bigger and change, the weather changes. People change their cars and their TVs. Teachers change. It's not always the same football team that is at the top of the Premier league or the same pop song that tops the charts. Things have certainly changed since your grandparents were your age. And if you have grandchildren things will be very different for them.

The poem suggests that it isn't only the fact of change that stays the same. God is always the same – always loving, always forgiving, always caring, always there for you. Little wonder that the person who wrote the psalms described God as a rock, something enduring, solid, always there (see Psalms 18:2; 31:3; 42:9; 71:3).

1. What things do you have that your Granny and Granddad didn't have?

2. Do you think life was as happy when they were young?

3. What things never change?

FIFTY

People see things this way

People see things this way;
people see them that.
Some accept a point of view;
some reject it flat.

Think you've all the answers?
Wait for a surprise.
Those who know they haven't,
they are truly wise.

Sometimes people argue;
drive themselves apart.
Don't refuse to differ:
that's how quarrels start.

Each have their opinions,
no doubt think them best.
Those who look for wisdom,
listen to the rest.

Learn from other people,
open up your mind.
Search for understanding,
see what you can find.

Nick Fawcett

Have a discussion in groups. It could be about anything: which country
is best at rugby?; what's the best film?; there should be more art lessons
in school; burgers are better than fish and chips. Different people will
have different views. If people feel very strongly about their own

opinion then an argument can start that can get very heated. But some discussions aren't just about opinions, they are ways of finding out new knowledge – like what caused the Second World War. The chances are that different people will still have different ideas but no one will have all the answers. Being willing to listen to other people and not thinking you know it all is an important way to learn.

1. What do you think is the difference between arguing and differing?

2. How far do you feel people listen to your point of view?

3. How do you feel when people argue with you?

4. Is being 'open' the same as simply ditching your own view and accepting that of someone else?

FIFTY-ONE

Prayer's like talking on a mobile phone

Prayer's like talking on a mobile phone,
make a call and God will listen.
If you're in a crowd or on your own,
use prayer like a mobile phone.

You can ring if you are worried,
if problems you must share.
You can call to shout out, 'Thank you, Lord,
for always being there.'

You can ring if you are sleepy,
or when you're wide awake.
And you know that he will answer you
whatever calls you make.

You will never need a contract,
a top-up or a PIN.
You can speak to God, the call is free.
You'll know that he'll be in!

Val Hawthorne

We often think that prayer is just about asking God for things: a new bike, fine weather for a day out, help with a test. But that is only part of what prayer is about. We don't talk to one another just to ask for things. We tell them what we've been doing, we thank them for helping us or giving us a present, we tell them how good they are if they do something well. Sometimes we just chat about nothing in particular. It's just nice to have someone to talk to.

Prayer is having a chat with God – about anything you like. But it is also about listening. It's not a proper conversation if only one person talks. Listening to God means just being quiet. Some people feel that God speaks to them when they read the Bible.

1. In what ways is prayer like a conversation and how does it differ?

2. God will always listen but do you think he always answers?

FIFTY-TWO

Reach for the sky

Reach for the sky and you, you can do anything.
Reach for the sky and you're, you're flying free.
Reach for the sky and you, you can be anyone.
Reach for the sky and be a star!
Reach for the sky and be a star!

And if the things you try seem impossible,
don't give up, don't give up.
Because anything can be possible
if you reach for the sky.

Ali Dee

Trying something new can be quite daunting. You feel uncertain. You might not be able to do it. You might fail. You might not like it. You might look silly. Others might encourage you: 'You can do it. Just have a go.' Having a go is better than doing nothing. You might surprise yourself – you might prove to be very good at something you have never tried before.

Discuss together what you would like to do when you grow up.

1. Are you satisfied with what you can do or would you like to do other things?

2. What help would you need?

3. How do you feel about trying again and again?

What do you think?

FIFTY-THREE

'Roar, roar,' said the lion

'Roar, roar,' said the lion.
'Squelch, squelch,' said the slug.
'Ooh, Ooh,' said the monkey,
'Crawl, crawl,' said the bug.
'Think, think,' said the world,
'I give these for free,
so treat me with care
for you owe them to me.'

'Hiss, hiss,' said the snake.
'Dig, dig,' said the mole.
'Drip, drip,' said the rain.
'Squeak, squeak,' said the vole.
'Think, think,' said the world,
'how dull and how poor
your lives would become
if you had these no more.'

'Splash, splash,' said the sea.
'Woof, woof,' said the dog.
'Gush , gush,' said the river.
'Croak, croak,' said the frog.
'Think, think,' said the world,
'of all you enjoy,
and save it for all –
don't waste and destroy.'

'Howl, howl,' said the wolf.
'Sing, sing,' said the lark.
'Creep, creep,' said the tortoise,
'Snap, snap,' said the shark.

'Think, think,' said the world,
'how sad it would feel
if creatures like these
were no longer real.'

'Tweet, tweet,' said the bird.
'Buzz, buzz,' said the bee.
'Bloom, bloom,' said the flower.
'Grow, grow,' said the tree.
'Think, think,' said the world,
'reflect on all these,
and treat me with care –
look after me, please.'

Nick Fawcett

In the last 100 years these ten animals became extinct: Californian grizzly bear, Newfoundland wolf, Tasmanian and Bali tigers, Guam flying fox, Cuban ivory-billed woodpecker, Jamaican Giant Galliwasp (lizard), Zanzibar leopard, Baiji (river dolphin from China), Pyrenean Ibex. They have gone for ever – like the Dodo.

Some of them have disappeared because they were hunted until none were left – like the grizzly bear. For others it was because their source of food declined – like the wolf when there were less and less caribou around. Cutting down trees meant that the woodpeckers had nowhere to go. What other reasons might there be?

1. Why does the world want you to take care of all the things mentioned in the poem?

2. How would it feel if there were no flowers, no animals, no birds?

3. What can you do to help look after the world?

FIFTY-FOUR

Some are full of action

Some are full of action and others like to dream.
Some are good at football and always make the team.
Some love writing stories, they build castles in the air.
For we all have special talents, we all have special talents,
we all have special talents God has given us to share.

Some are quick with numbers and others run for miles.
Some might have green fingers or simply make you smile!
Some play the guitar and others love to sing the blues.
For we all have special talents, we all have special talents,
we all have special talents God has given us to use.

Some are patient and others really kind.
Some can always tell when you've got something on your mind.
Some are just the kind of friend that everyone would choose.
For we all have special talents, we all have special talents,
we all have special talents God has given us to use.

Alison Carver

In a football team the goal keeper does not have to have the forward's talent to score goals. But a forward might be hopeless at keeping goal or being a defender. A good team has people in it with different skills and talents. The manager has to find out what each player is best at.

Discuss the different talents that there are in your class (or group). Everyone has something that they are good at.

1. What is your special talent?

2. How do you share and use your talent?

3. Are TV talent shows a good idea?

What do
you think?

FIFTY-FIVE

Some people say, 'The world's too small'

Some people say, 'The world's too small
and soon there'll be no space at all.
We've far too many children here,
and that's the future people fear.'
But hungry children still survive
and say, 'I'm poor but still alive.'
They look in dustbins every day
and eat the food we've thrown away.

The politicians said, 'It's clear
a global famine could be near.
If we can't grow more oats and wheat,
we'll soon have nothing left to eat.'
The farmer said, 'What shall I do?
As no one wants the crops I grew,
there's too much food in every store;
they've told me that they need no more.'

The soldiers said, 'We may be poor,
but we need guns to fight our war.
We don't buy hungry children bread,
but spend it all on war instead.'
And Jesus said, 'Why can't you see
all people are the same to me?
If you can make all nations one,
there will be food for everyone.'

Denis O'Gorman

It can be very confusing. Some people say there isn't enough food for everyone in the world and yet others say that in some countries there is so much food that lots of it is getting thrown away.

We are told that too many countries are too poor to ensure their people have good housing, good health services, enough food. But on average, countries throughout the world spend about £100 for every person each year on armaments.

1. What do you think prevents everyone having enough to eat?

2. What can be done about it?

3. What could you do about it?

4. In what ways are we wasteful?

FIFTY-SIX

Someone in the world is hungry

Someone in the world is hungry,
yet so many do not care.
Will we be the ones to help them?
Do we love enough to share?

Someone in the world is homeless,
far from country, far from friends.
Will we work with those who house them?
See that their dejection ends?

Someone in the world is hurting,
sick and suffering, left to die.
Will you try to ease their burden?
Not just look . . . then pass on by?

Someone in the world is needy,
poorer than we'll ever know.
Will we work to end injustice?
Will we let compassion show?

Someone in the world is broken,
tortured, beaten, racked with pain.
Will we work to help protect them?
Save them from that fate again?

Someone in the world is always
seeking help in their despair.
Will we be the ones who hear them?
Have we truly learnt to share?

Nick Fawcett

Here are some rather frightening statistics.

- There are nearly 800 million people in the world who do not have enough to eat. That's over ten times as many people as live in the whole of England. Most of them live in Asia. Nearly half of all children who die under the age of five, die of hunger.

- In 2014 there were 13 million refugees in the world.

- In England nearly three thousand people sleep out rough every night.

- About 120 countries use torture.

- In England about 4.6 million are in persistent poverty.

- Nearly half the people in the world live on less than £2 a day.

1. Consider just one of the verses in the poem: find out more about people in the situation described. What could you do to help?

2. What would you have to give up to be as poor as the poorest?

3. What would you take with you if you had to walk to another country as a refugee?

4. What would it feel like to be a refugee fleeing from war?

5. Which of Jesus' stories tells of people who looked at a person in need and then passed by?

FIFTY-SEVEN

Someone near is hurting

Someone near is hurting,
more than they can bear,
seeking help and comfort,
looking everywhere.
Will you show compassion?
Won't you just be there?
Focus more on others –
show the world you care.

Thousands more are hurting,
tearing out their hair,
overwhelmed by problems,
driven to despair.
Will you show compassion?
Won't you hear their prayer?
Focus more on others –
show the world you care.

Multitudes are hurting,
kitchen cupboards bare;
weak, deprived and starving –
life just isn't fair.
Will you show compassion?
Won't you learn to share?
Focus more on others –
show the world you care.

Nick Fawcett

The newspapers and the TV news are full of the suffering in the world. It can sometimes feel overwhelming and we just don't know what to do. But it is possible to do something about those people whom we know. It isn't just physical pain that hurts. Being lonely, or ignored or bullied can be very painful. Discuss how you feel when you 'hurt' and no one tries to help.

1. How do you feel about all the suffering there is?
2. What do you think you could do about it?
3. What is meant by 'compassion'?
4. What might you give up to help someone else?

FIFTY-EIGHT

Sometimes my head is busy and buzzy (Heartbeat)

Sometimes my head is busy and buzzy,
life around me's too fast and too fuzzy.
My mind's a muddle, my day's in a whirl,
and I don't know the answer to anything.
Then something says, 'Stop!'

Notice the butterfly,
gentle and light on the wing.
So much to do today,
yet peaceful and quiet and still,
I have inside me the peace that I need,
if I stop and I listen to a single heartbeat.

Sometimes my heart is beating too quickly,
I feel afraid and my legs feel like jelly.
Sums are confusing, my writing's a mess,
and I don't know the answer to anything.
Then something says, 'Stop!'

Ali Dee

It is nice to have lots of friends around you – always chatting, doing things together. But sometimes it is good to get away and just be on your own for a while. It can help to sort things out in your head when there are so many things to think about. Many schools have a place where you can go just to be quiet.

1. What do you do when you feel all in a muddle, life is all fuzzy?

2. Is there somewhere you can go to be quiet?

3. What reminds you to be peaceful, still and quiet?

FIFTY-NINE

Stuff!

In my bedroom I've got lots of stuff,
sometimes I think I haven't got enough.
I've got a lot but then there seem to be
lots of people who are not like me.

You can play it or ride it,
you can eat it or hide it.
You can watch it or wear it,
spend it or share it.

I've got a lot of stuff and so have you,
there's lots of people who will need things too.
All give a little bit and when that's done,
there'll be enough to share with everyone.

Some people have enough and some have not,
I think that you and me have got a lot.
Let's think of everyone and make things fair,
there's such a lot of stuff that we can share.

Sarah Watts

'Stuff' means all those things we have, we own. It doesn't include those things we eat and drink. Some people have tried to live more simply with less 'stuff'. They sell or give away most of what they have and live with just 50 or 100 pieces of 'stuff' – and that includes furniture, cutlery, crockery, clothes. What do you think of that?

Do you have anything that you haven't used for over two months? Do you need it? Would you miss it if it disappeared or if you gave it away?

1. If the house were on fire what 'stuff' would you want to save?

2. What's the difference between what you want and what you need?

3. How could you share some of your 'stuff'?

4. What would you like someone to share with you?

SIXTY

There are lots of things (It's good to be me!)

There are lots of things
that it's good to be.
It's good to be kind
and it's very, very good to be me!

It's good to be gentle, it's good to be fair,
it's good to be funny and it's good to share!

It's good to be helpful, it's good to be there,
it's good to be laughing and it's good to care!

Ali Dee

The good things we can be are sometimes called virtues and the bad things are called vices. The ancient Greeks said that there were four key virtues: justice, prudence (wisely cautious), temperance (moderation) and courage. Christians added three more: faith, hope, and love.

Vices are ways that we consistently behave that are damaging or hurtful. A famous writer called Dante made a list of seven of what he felt were the worst vices: Pride, envy (jealousy), anger (hatred), laziness, greed, gluttony, and lust.

1. How many of the good things are you?

2. How glad are you to be 'you'?

3. Would you like to make any changes?

4. What do other people think of you?

What do
you think?

SIXTY-ONE

There's a man we see in town

There's a man we see in town,
just standing on street corners,
all alone, he has no home.
Though, perhaps, we walk on by
and think he's not our problem,
he's still there, and we all should care.

Don't judge others by where they live,
or by the clothes they're wearing.
Don't judge others by what they say or do.
We should try to understand or lend a helping hand.
Don't judge others, or others might judge you!

If a friend says hurtful words
or does things that are spiteful,
would we stay, or walk away?
Deep down they might need a friendly
shoulder they can cry on.
Life is tough, they're not strong enough.

If someone is not the same,
some people think they're wrong,
that they are strange, and they must change.
But the world is colourful
'cos everyone is different
and that's great, let's celebrate.

Alison Carver

It is right to be cautious about strangers. Not everyone is a good person. Some people can do bad things. But just because someone is different doesn't mean they are bad. They may look strange, they may talk oddly, they might live in a strange place but that doesn't make them bad.

Consider all the differences there are among the other children in your class. How do you feel about those differences? How might the differences be celebrated?

1. How do you react to people who are different or strange?

2. What is the difference between judging and prejudice?

3. Why might a friend say nasty things to you?

SIXTY-TWO

There's a word

There's a word, a little word,
and it's sometimes hard to say it.
Do you know that little word?
One we often need to say.
Say it when we've been all cross,
not done as we should.
'Sorry' is that little word,
helps to make a bad day good.

There's a word, a little word,
and it's sometimes hard to say it.
But we need that little word,
need to say it every day.
Say it when we've been unkind,
when we've hurt a friend.
'Sorry' is that little word,
makes things better in the end.

There's a word, a little word,
and it's sometimes hard to say it.
But we need that little word,
need to say it when we pray.
God will hear a quiet prayer,
putting wrong things right.
'Sorry' is that little word,
helps to make a dark day bright.

Val Hawthorne

We all make mistakes. We all can do things that hurt or upset others – sometimes without meaning to but sometimes on purpose. It doesn't take much effort to be nasty. It can be much more difficult to say sorry. But if we don't, things can get worse. There are members of some families who have not spoken to each other for years because of something that was said and no one said sorry. You can lose a good friend just because you won't say sorry. Just a small word but it means so much, makes such a difference.

1. Why is it sometimes hard to say 'sorry'?

2. Are we always prepared to forgive someone if they say sorry to us?

3. How do we know that God forgives us when we say 'sorry'?

SIXTY-THREE

There's too much hurting, too many tears

There's too much hurting, too many tears,
too many burdens, too many fears,
too much hunger and far too much need,
too much injustice, too much greed.

There's too much sickness, too much despair,
too much misfortune, too few who care,
too much anger and way too much pride,
too many broken deep inside.

There's too much envy, too much hate,
too many people left to their fate;
too much killing – oh what's it all for? –
too much division, too much war.

We can't work wonders, right every wrong,
solve every problem – we're not that strong –
can't do magic, or brandish a wand;
but what we *can* do is respond.

The world needs healing, making anew.
It starts with people like me and you.
Hear them crying. Oh, what can we give?
How can *I* help them . . . help them live?

Nick Fawcett

The amount of pain and suffering in the world can seem to be so great that we wonder if anything we do could make the slightest difference. On our own there is so little that we can do to solve the suffering of refugees, to feed all the starving children in Africa, to stop the killing in the Middle East. But because we cannot do everything it doesn't mean we can't do something. And when lots of people do a bit then it can make a real difference. A lot of charities begin with just one person wanting to make a difference and getting others to join in.

1. How far is the world still a good place in spite of the 'bad' things that happen?

2. Choose one of the 'bad' things and think how you could respond to help.

3. Why do you think God doesn't stop all the 'bad' things?

SIXTY-FOUR

This is the place where we are safe and free (School song)

This is the place where we are safe and free
to play and be with others
who make us feel that we are special too.

We've friends to play with and fun to share,
love and kindness are everywhere,
and all around us are those who care;
our laughter always fills the air.

We're really proud of the things we do,
we are proud of each other too.
We read and count and we skip and run;
our learning fills our days with fun.

Ali Dee

The teachers and governors of your school have the responsibility for making sure you are safe in school. The buildings must be kept in good order, equipment must be inspected to ensure it is not dangerous, the grounds of the school are fenced to keep you safe. There are rules about not running in school and how medicines are to be kept and administered. Sometimes rules can feel annoying but when they are there to keep you safe it is important everyone keeps them.

1. How safe do you feel in school?

2. Do you help to make others feel special?

3. What makes school fun?

SIXTY-FIVE

Though we come from different places

Though we come from different places,
though we each have different faces,
though we make up different races –
live in peace.

Though we've different ways of seeing,
though we've different ways of being,
though we argue – disagreeing –
live in peace.

Let us learn to love each other,
seeing all as sister, brother;
let our broken world recover –
live in peace.

In a world that needs repairing,
let us try our hands at sharing,
changing hearts and minds through caring –
live in peace.

Nick Fawcett

Some of the troubles in the Middle East, in places like Syria and Iraq, are the result of quarrels lasting many centuries. For a while, people seem to be able to live in peace but then the arguments break out again. Sometimes it is about questions of religion, sometimes it is about who is in charge, sometimes a bit of both. Families, towns, countries can be split because people will not live in peace with difference. If every individual was willing to live in peace – there would be no war. It all starts with you.

1. Why does being different so often cause trouble?

2. How would you help people to live in peace with those who are different?

3. Who do you know who is different from you? How do you treat them?

SIXTY-SIX

Try, try, try it again

Have you ever wondered what it's like to see
if you could be smarter than you used to be?
You can do so many things especially when,
you can try, try, try it again.

Go on, give it a go,
if you don't you won't find out,
you'll never know.
So now, give it a try,
otherwise you'll spend your life
just wondering why.

Have you ever wondered what it's like to run
just a little faster than you've always done?
You can do so many things especially when,
you can try, try, try it again.

Have you ever wondered if you ever should
be a bit more patient than you always could?
You can do so many things especially when,
you can try, try, try it again.

Have you ever wondered if it's time to do
lots of different things that might be new to you?
You can do so many things especially when,
you can try, try, try it again.

Sarah Watts

Robert the Bruce was King of Scotland and a great warrior. He led his people in wars against the English. There is a famous legend about him. Things had not been going well and in the winter of 1306-07, Bruce was hiding in a cave on small island. He noticed a small spider spinning a web, trying to connect the thread between two parts of the cave's roof. Two of its attempts failed. But the spider did not give up. It tried a third time and succeeded. Bruce decided to try again and he returned to battle against the English. He succeeded and eventually gained independence for Scotland.

1. Trying again and again takes effort and can feel risky. Why do some people think it is worth the effort? Do you?

2. What new thing would you like to try to do?

3. Is doing new things exciting or frightening – or a bit of both?

4. What happens if you never try, try again?

SIXTY-SEVEN

What shall I do with today?

What shall I do with today?
Will it be a day of making changes?
What will come my way?
I wonder what things will make my day.

It's my day, and only I
can make it the best I can.
Think of all the things that just could be
the start of something good!

What shall I do with today?
Will it be a day of trying harder?

What shall I do with today?
Will it be a day of making new friends?

What shall I do with today?
Will it be a day of being patient?

What shall I do with today?
Will it be a day of helping others?

What shall I do with today?
Will it be a day of listening harder?

What shall I do with today?
Will it be a day of being quiet?

What shall I do with today?
Will it be a day of being bolder?

Sarah Watts

Every day is new. Today has never happened before. There are always some things we do every day. We wake up, we get up (unless we are ill), we get dressed. We eat, we talk, we walk, we play. There will be lessons when we are at school. We will meet other children. A lot feels the same. But we can still choose to do something different, something new. The poem suggests some of the things you could do with today.

1. Does each new day feel like a day when something good could happen, or a day when everything will just be the same?

2. What new thing will you try today for yourself, for someone else?

3. How do you feel about today?

SIXTY-EIGHT

When a challenge starts off easy

When a challenge starts off easy
but then turns out to be tough;
when you thought a test was simple
but the going ends up rough;
keep on trying, keep on trying,
keep your spirits up my friend;
keep on trying, keep on trying,
and you'll get there in the end.

When you set off bright and breezy
but you wind up out of puff;
when you summon every effort,
but it doesn't prove enough;
keep on trying, keep on trying,
keep your spirits up my friend;
keep on trying, keep on trying,
and you'll get there in the end.

When you think you've solved a problem
but the answer turns out duff;
when you try to write an epic,
but produce a load of guff;
keep on trying, keep on trying,
keep your spirits up my friend;
keep on trying, keep on trying,
and you'll get there in the end.

When you're told you could do better
don't go getting in a huff;
don't go giving the impression
that you couldn't give a stuff;

keep on trying, keep on trying,
keep your spirits up my friend;
keep on trying, keep on trying,
and you'll get there in the end.

Nick Fawcett

Have you ever run a race and you started really fast but before the end you were out of breath and your legs just didn't seem to want to go? Did you give up – or keep trying even harder? It's not easy. If things are more difficult than we expect it takes determination not to get down and fed up. Giving up is easy, keeping on trying is tough, but worth it.

1. How do you feel when people say you could do better?

2. How do other people feel if you go off in a huff?

3. Who do you think could help you if you want to keep trying?

SIXTY-NINE

When I fail to be the person

When I fail to be the person
truly I intend;
when my words and deeds are different –
will you be my friend?
When I'm grumpy, even angry;
when my words offend;
when I'm greedy, mean and selfish –
will you be my friend?

When I've spoken words that hurt you;
words I can't defend;
will you trust I didn't mean them –
will you be my friend?
When I'm silly, careless, thoughtless;
drive you round the bend;
will you see beneath the surface –
will you be my friend?

When I quarrel, cause a break-up
sometimes hard to mend,
will you let me say I'm sorry –
will you be my friend?
When your faith in me is broken,
patience at an end;
though I've let you down so often –
will you be my friend?

Nick Fawcett

'A friend,' the saying goes, 'is someone who knows all about you but is still your friend.' Many of the things about each one of us are very good. Most of the time you try to be the sort of person people want to be friends with. But there are times when you are not – you can be grumpy or moody or impatient or quarrelsome. Even with a friend. A good friend knows what you can be like – good and bad, but still wants to be your friend. Are you a good friend like that?

1. Would you be willing to be a friend to someone who treated you like this?

2. Why do we let our friends down in these ways?

3. Is there someone who is always your friend no matter what you do?

SEVENTY

When I feel nervous,
when I feel scared
(Friendship)

When I feel nervous, when I feel scared,
needing some caring, you have been there,
holding my hand ...

> *and guiding me through*
> *this land of strange emotions;*
> *you have been there,*
> *you have been there,*
> *you have been there.*

When I've been smiling, having some fun,
sharing the laughter, you've been the one,
taking my hand ...

When I've been angry, misunderstood,
needing some calming, you've been so good,
touching my hand ...

Ali Dee

Some people enjoy feeling a little bit scared. Perhaps you do. They watch a film which they know has a scary bit in it and although they scream they still watch. Or they go on a ride at the funfair that races up and down or swings round and round. It can be a bit frightening but enjoyable as well. But sometimes being frightened is not fun. It feels horrible. And then it's good to have a friend to be with you.

Having fun on your own can be fine but it's better when you have a friend to share it with.

Getting all upset and angry can go on and on for ages. But it helps to have a friend just to be with you and calm you down.

1. Who is your best friend? Are they always there for you?

2. How does it feel when you fall out with your friend?

3. When was Jesus deserted by his friends?

4. Do you think something can be scary and enjoyable at the same time?

SEVENTY-ONE

When Jesus was my age

When Jesus was my age he played with his friends,
played with his friends, played with his friends;
when Jesus was my age he played with his friends
and he's friends with each one of us now.

When Jesus was my age he laughed and sang,
he laughed and sang, he laughed and sang,
when Jesus was my age he laughed and sang,
and he loves hearing us singing now.

When Jesus was my age he sometimes felt sad,
he sometimes felt sad, he sometimes felt sad,
when Jesus was my age he sometimes felt sad,
and he shares in our sadness now.

When Jesus was my age he went to school,
he went to school, he went to school,
when Jesus was my age he went to school,
and he goes everywhere with us now.

Susan Sayers

Jesus is such an important person and he lived on earth so long ago we sometimes forget that in so many ways he was just like us. He did many of the things you do, he enjoyed some of the things you enjoy, he was sad sometimes like you are. Just because he didn't have a computer or a bicycle or a mobile phone doesn't mean he was so different he could not understand how you feel.

Because he is with you all the time he knows how you feel, he is your friend.

1. In what ways was Jesus' childhood like ours and in what ways was it different?

2. How aware are you of Jesus being with you?

3. What difference does it make to you to know Jesus is always with you?

SEVENTY-TWO

When someone shows a little act of kindness

When someone shows a little act of kindness,
a little deed of goodness,
a simple sign of niceness,
it's good to show it hasn't gone unnoticed,
that you value what they've done.

Thank you very much,
thank you very much,
thank you for the things you do.

When someone shows a little bit of caring,
a little bit of sharing,
concern when you're despairing,
it's good to show your thankfulness, declaring
that you value what they've done.

When someone offers help in times of sorrow,
brings hope to face tomorrow,
gives strength on which to borrow,
it's good to show their gesture wasn't hollow,
that you value what they've done.

When someone gives relief when you are tired,
compassion when required,
support when it's desired,
it's good to show their kindness has inspired,
that you value what they've done.

Nick Fawcett

If someone gave you a really nice birthday present would you just snatch it and say nothing? If someone rescued you from drowning would you just walk away and say nothing? If someone gave you a lift home when you missed the bus would you just dash off and say nothing? We usually remember to say 'thank you' for big things. But what about the smaller, everyday things? Any kindness deserves a 'thank you'.

1. Why is showing gratitude a good thing?

2. How does it feel if you do a kindness to someone and they don't thank you?

3. What ways are there of showing our gratitude other than by saying 'thank you'?

SEVENTY-THREE

When you're feeling nervous, when you're feeling scared

When you're feeling nervous, when you're feeling scared.
When you face a challenge greater than you've dared.
Try your best to face it, try to take it on.
Try to stand against it till the fear is gone.

Meet it, beat it, cheat it;
don't just hide away.
Face your terror bravely;
make it go away.

When you're feeling frightened, feel you cannot cope.
When you feel defeated, never give up hope.
Greet the problem squarely, take it on the chin.
Though you may not think so, finally you'll win.

Nick Fawcett

The really great heroes, the ones who are really brave aren't the ones who never feel scared, are never afraid. The true heroes are those who know they are frightened but still carry on. They are frightened of the dark but still go into a cave to help rescue someone. They don't like heights but walk to the edge of a cliff to save a child from falling over. They do what is right even though they feel frightened. They face their fear.

1. What are the things you fear most?

2. What do you do when you are afraid?

3. How would you help someone who said they were frightened?

4. Jesus must have been afraid when he knew he was going to die. What did he do?

SEVENTY-FOUR

Who cares for carers?

Who cares for carers
who work all night and day?
Lots of them are lonely folk,
from countries far away.
They work in all our hospitals
to take away our pain.
But some still say,
'Don't let them stay,
but send them back again.'

Who cares for carers,
who sometimes feel alone?
We get all their care and love,
then leave them on their own.
They work in all our nursing homes,
you'll find them everywhere.
But when they say,
'I too need love,'
does anybody care?

Who cares for carers,
or nurses from abroad?
Should we pay them
what they earn,
the country can't afford?
But when you go to hospital
and see them waiting there,
just say a prayer and
thank them all
that they still love and care.

Denis O'Gorman

It can be all too easy to take for granted those who care for the sick people in hospitals or the elderly people in care homes. After all, they get paid for it. But often they get paid very little. Many of them are far from their families and friends. Our hospitals and care homes would never have enough staff if they did not have people who come from overseas. They do not always get treated very well and that is wrong.

1. Where do most of the overseas carers come from?

2. What are the reasons that some are not paid properly?

3. Why do people say they should go back to where they came from?

SEVENTY-FIVE

Yes, the journey of life

Yes, the journey of life that we travel
has lots of adventures in store.
There's so much that we can learn about
and a wonderful world to explore.

Each day is a day we should treasure.
Let's fill it with laughter and joy.
'Cos we're moving on, moving on,
together we're moving on.
Yes, we're moving on, moving on,
together we're moving on.

On the journey of life that we travel
there are plenty of choices to make.
We will stand at crossroads on the way
and consider the road we should take.

On the journey of life that we travel,
we're walking with God by our side.
He will help us if the road is rough
and is always our friend and our guide.

Alison Carver

'It's been an amazing journey,' says the young pop star who has just had a Number 1 and was totally unknown a few months ago. She doesn't mean she's been travelling. The journey is all the things she has been doing, the changes that have happened to her, the choices she's made. It's a saying that is heard everywhere.

Life's a journey – from the day we were born to the day we die. Every day is part of that journey. Some days are great, others are pretty awful.

We don't have control over everything that happens. But there are many things we do have a choice about. Making the right choice makes a big difference to how the day turns out.

Some things that happen can upset us, can make us feel rotten but on this journey we are not alone. Having someone with you always helps – and God is always with you.

1. In what ways does your life feel like an adventure?

2. What are some of the choices you have to make?

3. What difference do you think it makes if God is always with you?

SEVENTY-SIX

You can't always have what you want

You can't always have what you want.
You may have to wait, you may have to wait.
If there's something you want right now,
you may have to wait, you may have to wait.

If the answer is 'no',
don't get in a strop,
or stamp your feet in anger
and don't blow your top.

Learn to be patient, learn what it means,
what you think you want isn't always what you need.
Learn to be patient, wait for the best,
you don't always have to be the same as all the rest.

Becky Silver

There are some things you cannot have immediately when you want them. If you find a flower in bud you have to wait until it flowers for you to see the full bloom. If you pick at the petals they will spoil. If you want a slice of the cake that has just gone in the oven you have to wait until it is cooked. If you want the number 33 bus you have to wait until it comes. Just jumping on the first bus when it is going the wrong way will not help.

When you really, really want something, being patient can be very difficult. But getting angry, or sulking, or jumping up and down doesn't make the bud flower any quicker, or the cake cook any quicker, or the bus come any quicker.

1. How do you feel when you have to wait for something you really want?

2. What difference does it make when the thing you want isn't something you need?

3. How much do you want things just because someone else has them?

4. Do you think God ever asks us to wait?

INDEX